Inspired Woman

A Collection of Passionate Poetry
By
Karen Godson

Riff Raff Press
Ontario, Canada
Copyright 2010

ISBN 0-9782516-0-1

For years, I was told by an ex-partner that my writing was a waste of time; that first books are NEVER published, and that no one reads poetry anymore.

I believe that all words are worth reading and every human being deserving of a chance to be heard. So in 2002, at the age of 38 I began the long journey towards fufilling my dream. I pulled all of my poems together into a manuscript, "Inspired Woman".
three separate books; one of Passionate Poetry, one of Dark Poetry, and one of Poems containing fewer than 20 words. Realizing that book publishers prefer an author with a track record, I submitted some of my poems to a few Canadian poetry magazines, anthologies and literary journals. Just a few months after I sent the first submission, I received a reply. Soon followed another, and another.

1 of my poems was published in Hammered Out, 2 in Quills Poetry Magazine, and more were chosen and featured in online poetry magazines. In February 2003 I was the Featured Poet on Creative Women, a site for women who write, paint and dream. I was also a featured poet in the Spring issue of Ascent Online Magazine. In November of 2004, I had multiple poems published in a book of poetry entitled "Lesbian Spirit-Words from Within" and 4 more in "Lust", an anthology of erotic works by many talented Canadian poets; published by William Byron

Sheardown. 2 pieces appeared in The Real Eight View Issue 5, and still others in the April Issue of Ascent Online Magazine. 2 poems were published in "New Classic Poems", a First Edition anthology by the founder of "Contemporary Formal Poetry" Neil Harding McAlister. 3 years after my first submission, I appeared in Quills for the 3rd time, and was included in Grey Borders: Pop Culture Magazine!

Feeling suddenly very powerful, I went on to register myself as a publisher; "Riff Raff Press", Now with mighty pen in hand and a determination sharper than ever I am marching forward like an Amazon warrior... intent on publishing Inspired Woman!

And so I say to the above-mentioned ex...

"While you are busy eating your words, I'll continue writing mine!"

Amy's Song

Today I was inspired
by the music in my head.
I saw you dancing 'round and 'round
in ribbons pink and red.
You whirled and danced, and arabesqued
to music quite unheard,
then fluttered to me and alit
upon me as a little bird.

I brushed away a lock of hair
from out your carefree eyes;
you tossed your most enchanting head
and took off for the skies.
I watched you go, and felt a pang.
Oh, how I wished you'd stay,
but yet I know I love you so
I left you to your play.

Fly...though the world is much too wide.
Sing...until you reach the other side.
Go...if you feel you have a dream.
I'll be waiting here for you,
if things aren't as they seem.

I know I will be sorry
for letting you go free,
but I will hold on to the dream

that you'll return one day to me.
And as I watch you go
I will wave a sad goodbye.
I know that this is what you need
so I won't let you see me cry.

Fly...though the world is much too wide.
Sing...until you reach the other side.
Go...if you feel you have a dream.
I'll be waiting here for you,
if things aren't as they seem.
Today, I was inspired
by the music in my head...

Anju

Velcro Spirit
holds me fast
clinging to me
like a new vine
up an old stone wall.
Ice blue eyes
sear your features
onto my soul.
Words have no meaning.
Silence holds secrets
that scream out to be heard.
I inhale your scent
committing it to memory,
filed in the slot marked
"Urgent".

Astral Projection

your silhouette is forever burned
onto the inside of My eyelids.
I study your face from across the room,
across the Universe,
so that your flawless features
are branded on My soul.
Your sizzling stare
burns hunger into My heart.
The mist that is My essence
drifts across the floor,
pressing its moist ghost-mouth to yours.
Tasting your curiosity,
smelling your arousal,
feeling your quivering,
knowing your longing,
I ease back into My body;
into consciousness.
your eyes, still staring,
tell of a knowing,
a secret,
that says I reached you.

Before You

Before you,
there were thorns without roses;
rain without rainbows; birds without song.
There used to be bees but no honey;
grapes but no wine;
night time but no sunset.
Before you,
my heart simply beat out of necessity,
counting down the seconds
I had been allotted on this Earth.
Then I saw you, and the sky caught fire;
songbirds chimed like Cathedral Bells;
rainbows danced across the sky,
dripping pure color onto newly opened roses.
Now I feast on your honey;
I am intoxicated by your wine.
My head reels,
my heart drives on with Steam-engine intent.
It's only purpose now,
to beat as one with yours.

Be Still

If you were Mine,
if you were Mine I'd climb a ladder
and light every star
with the fire in My heart.

If you were Mine,
yes, if you were Mine I'd sail across the sea
and bring you back the rarest of flowers
from the farthest shore.

If you were Mine,
no, when you are Mine
I will taste only sweetness on your lips,
and hear only music from your heart.

You will last in My mind
as an etching in stone,
untouched by life's weathering storms.

We will grow old,
we will be still and quiet,
but we will be together.

Bumping into my Soul Mate

I tremble at the resemblance;
the reconnaissance
a renaissance.
The past in a glance,
a whirling dance;
hypnotic trance,
circumstance.
Memorized essence
recurring life sentence
invisible fence
present and past tense
reassemble, and hence,
again I tremble...

Cunning Linguist

I stand three feet behind you
watching you type and
seeing that place on
your neck where
your hair stops
and your collar starts.
I want to shove
My face into it and
smell you and feel your
shivers when My hot breath
gives you goose bumps.
My mind traces
an invisible finger
around the front and
over your throat.
I can feel you swallow
when My touch makes you
catch your breath.
I am thinking about your
naked, herbal-essence skin
melting under My finger.
Now, I am walking
around to the front of you;
seeing your look
of sudden surprise
and then cunning
when you realize I have

silently become naked too.
you didn't hear Me
undressing just behind you;
your constant typing
kept My secret.
But now,
the Cat's out of the bag
hehehe, so to speak.
I am a nude sculpture,
in the dark behind My eyelids,
as your hands close
around My Ivory hips.
you are pulling Me
towards you
your eyes raised to meet Mine,
then lowered again
to map out your Route.
The smirk crouching in the corners
of your mouth
reminds Me of a hungry hyena.
All I can do
is place My hands
on your shoulders,
so My knees don't betray Me.
And I stand here,
your dessert,
while you type.

Did I Forget To Mention?

You may not have known
when I gave you My heart
that it came with a promise
" Til death us do part."
My love is forever;
I've willed it to you.
Don't ask, " Do you love me? "
Just know that I DO.

I may not have told you
that you make Me whole.
You fill all the spaces
I had in My soul.
I become more complete
with each hole that you fill.
Don't ask, " Will You be there?"
Just know that I WILL.

Drug Of Choice

So what if I
slip into your mind;
make you leave it all behind?
Is that so bad?

If you let Me in
I can get under your skin.
Throw your caution to the wind.
I could make you bad.

I want to be the drug
you never get enough of.
Inject Me, trip on Me,
Jones for My love.

Come on take Me under.
Your pulse is like thunder.
I can feel your red-hot hunger.
Let Me make you bad.

I can be the drug
you never get enough of.
Inject Me, trip on Me.
Jones for My love.

I want to make you
Jones for My love.

Excite Me

Excite Me, just by looking at Me.
Go ahead. I dare you.
You don't know what it does to Me.
I could drop from the face of the Earth,
and die, never knowing
the feeling was mutual.
Or, I could show you Life
and love, and maybe you'd know then
what it is like to be starving for something
that tastes like Everything
you have ever had a craving for.
I'll die if I never get to feed your craving,
and taste your need.
But for now, I'll just ask you one small thing.
Excite Me.
Just by looking at Me.

Future Holdings

I want so badly to touch you
and brush back the hair from your eyes.
Oh, how I so long to kiss you,
and melt that courageous disguise.
So close to Me that I can taste you
yet never quite so far away;
My only desire, to hold you;
My only fear, that you won't stay.
Perhaps if I brush up against you
your shoulder or maybe your arm,
you'll assume that it wasn't on purpose
and see that I mean you no harm.
All that I ask is the present
but pray for a future, that 's true.
I honestly don't want a future
at all if it doesn't hold you.

Garden Fountain

I should turn to stone;
carve Myself into the image
of a Goddess
so that you have no choice
but to gaze upon Me
in awe and reverence.
I should place a spell on you
so that all you see is Me,
in every ripple in the pond,
every voluptuous cloud,
in every strange woman's face.
you will pine for Me
as you touch My cold body;
long for a pulse,
a breath,
a kiss.
But instead, I will give you
a salty, glistening fountain,
flowing from My gray granite eyes.

Goddess Bless Tim Horton

Every morning on the train,
I watch her
methodically spreading
strawberry jam on her
muesli bagel
with a plastic knife.
Clenched between her thighs,
her hot
double-double awaits
its turn at her
sweet lips.
A jerk and a bump
and the lucky strawberry jam
is spread across her
already delicious palm.
I want to offer to lick it off
but it's too damned early
in the morning
to have a jam handprint
on My face.

Haiku Quartet

Lazy afternoon
drifting in and out of sleep
wrapped up in your smile

Navy blue plaid sheets
tangled mass of skin and cloth
arms and legs entwined

Shall I tell you now
of desire moist as dew
on My morning grass?

Rest your tired head
other days will come and go
better for the wait

Having You Here

I can smell you on My sheets.
If I close My eyes, I can see you
lying beside Me;
I can feel your back against My breast,
rising and falling.
I hear you moan as you dream,
perhaps of Me.
But of these false comforts,
none is as sweet as the taste of your velvet lips,
and that is the one thing I most hunger for,
yet cannot conjure.
I need you here right now,
to remind Me of how very sweet you taste.
Because no matter how hard I try,
nothing I do can even come close
to having you here.

Head Over Heels

I know the sensible thing to do
would be to turn and walk away;
to scold My heart for once again
allowing Me to fall
head over heels,
mind over matter,
ass over tea kettle.
The easy thing to do
would be to hurt her so badly
that she has to be the one to stop this.
The right thing to do
would be to tell her everything, now.
The crazy thing to do
would be to ignore
the sensible, easy, right things,
and let Myself fall
head over heels,
mind over matter,
ass over tea kettle.
So call Me crazy.
Guilty by reason of insanity!

In My Wildest Dreams

In My wildest dreams
I never thought I would find you.
Do you know how many lifetimes I have searched,
knowing you were out there somewhere
searching for Me too?
your skin is just as I remember it.
So soft; so warm.
your hairs smells just as I knew it would.
your beautiful eyes laugh at Me;
entice Me;
excite Me.
your face shines for Me.
your voice sings to Me like an angel.
Every inch, sound, smell, touch,
part of you
is exactly as I remember it,
in My wildest dreams.

Intimidation

Forgive me for my eager tongue
that only wants to taste,
yet cannot form a single word.
Forgive me for my haste.

It's just that You, a Goddess,
who wears a golden crown,
are quite aware that You could make
my sky come crashing down.

Irresistible

Take the tie from 'round the curtain
and let it fall to hide
the mingling of our playfulness
from the world outside.

Let not mere stranger see our bliss
nor robin spy our game,
but let My fantasies alight
on the whispering of your name.

Is It So Hard?

It seems as though My love for her
has reached its fullness,
and I can't imagine having room
for any more.
But then she comes to Me,
and My heart reassures Me that indeed
it has more for her
than even I knew.
Just having her beside Me,
knowing she wants to be with Me
is enough to live on.
Why do others ask so much of her,
when all they have to do is give
everything they have to her,
and she will be happy?
If the only thing I ever achieve
is to make her feel loved,
appreciated, wanted, understood,
Then I will die fulfilled.

Keeping It Simple

How tormenting
to bite My tongue;
smile a hollow smile,
and act as though we're best of friends,
yearning for her all the while.
I pine, I need,
I crave, I mourn,
yet am halfway consoled
by her graceful beauty,
that quiets My restless soul.
I'm damned to see
her halo and
her opalescent wings;
to hear angelic music
from her sweet voice as she sings.
I cannot touch
her heavenly body,
it is far too divine.
Suffice it then
to be the only one
who knows she's Mine.

Knick Knack

Tucked away in a corner curio cabinet,
covered with a layer of dust,
so unnoticed by the majority,
yet so sought after by those
who know your true beauty.
By stripping away the debris
and years of neglect
they would see the intense, unmatched
artistry that is you.
But most are not willing
to put forth the effort
it takes to know and understand
the true magnificence that lies
buried in the corner.
I am willing.
I will wipe away the years
and let your awesome light shine.
And pray that you'll shine it on Me.

Morning Breaks

Against My will
I escape the dark;
The glistening velvet moon
Sparkling as wine
Emblazoning your skin.

A whispering wind
tickles the rosebushes,
fluttering through the leaves
with the illusion of
tiny wings.

Morning breaks
with heavy fragrance,
My heart given up
to the mystique of you
and your dawn-softened face.

My Goddess

Your cool finger traces
a path down my neck,
over my throat,
'til I catch my breath
at the slightest touch
of Your heavenly hand.
Your will is my absolute,
total command.
I surrender my heart
to Your comforting arms;
entranced by Your eyes
and Goddess-like charms.
And I shall be happy
to sit at Your feet
when each beat of my heart cries
" Complete. Complete. "

Nothing

Not mountains of pine trees
that tickle the sky;
not earth-cleaving canyons
with walls two miles high;
not fathoms of oceans
that caress the cool sand;
nothing compares to the touch of your hand.
Not thunderous storm clouds
that black out the sun;
not the cry of a baby
who's life's just begun;
not having all three of
My wishes come true;
nothing's as awesome as being with you.

Pressed Flower

I pressed a flower to My lips
and closed My eyes;
imagined your mouth caressing Mine;
inhaled the fragrance, made a mental note
that you smell better
than any rose
that ever tickled My nose,
or rosehips
that ever graced These lips.
you feel better than any velvet petal
on satin skin.
you taste better
than the sweetest honey there has ever been.
And your name in My ears
sounds better than
the birds at sunrise, as dark disappears.
When I pressed this flower to My mouth,
I thought I'd like
to guide it South,
to come to rest
on mounds moist with dew,
and imagined its gentle caresses were you.

Religion

In the dark I watch you
dancing on your own;
sweat glistening on your body.
Can I take you home?
Drums pound out the rhythm,
throbbing, burning fire.
Mesmerized by your motion,
wet with sweat and desire.
your eyes look right through Me,
to the one against the wall.
I know he'll only hurt you.
Can I catch you when you fall?
Jesus! you're a goddess!
you're so damned divine.
you think you want Adonis,
but I can change your mind.
Let Me worship you,
surrender to you.
Sacrifice Myself to you.
Let Me worship you.
I'll lie across your altar,
say a prayer or two,
then I'll get down on My knees
and give My all to you.
I'll read you sacred verses,
tell you you're the chosen one,
then I'll teach you the meaning

of speaking in tongue.
Let Me worship you...

She Plays The Flute

Note by note
The flute sings its joyful song.
Music emerges like a butterfly,
stretching its wings
and floating on the breeze.
I hang on every note she plays,
as if each were a thread
connecting My soul to hers.
When I see her smile
And her eyes dance,
I long to hear those notes again.
I see her in My head
when I close My eyes,
And I softly whisper,
" Play for Me".

Snow Angel

My eyes trickle over your sculpted hips
like cool spring water caressing
sun-warmed river rocks.
I marvel at the purity
of your ivory skin.
your body,
so long untouched
is flawless like the landscape
after a midnight snowfall.
I want to walk across it
with feather-light fingertips;
careful to leave no blemish,
no sign I was ever here.
Only,
we would know.

So Much More

Look at Me.
I'm a mess.
I can't think of a time
when I wanted a woman so much
but was so willing to wait for her.
How can I not have her?
If I don't tell her how much I need her,
how much I'm starving for her,
she'll never know.
God, why does this
have to be so complicated?
If it was just sex
I could say,
"Hey baby, let Me buy you a drink."
And get it over with.
But it's not just sex. Not even close.
It's so much more
that I'm afraid to tell her
exactly what it is.
It's life-
and she's it.

Sweet Sapphonite

I want to feel her heart pounding with Mine.
I want to close My eyes
and feel her soft breath on My cheek.
I want to taste her;
to caress her with My tongue,
like a hummingbird savoring
the heavenly nectar of
the morning glory.
To drink in the warm dew,
and smell the fragrance of her flower.
I want to hear her sigh
as I give her everything
she longs for in life,
and I want to see her smile at Me
when she realizes I can give her
all this and so much more.
But above all, I want to tell her
I Love her,
and have her know just how much
I mean it.

The Kiss

she kissed Me last night.
Long, soft and full of promise.
At least it was on My end.
" I promise to love you
like I love life itself.
To be devoted to the cause,
true to your dreams,
faithful to your heart,
and to not ask for anything but the love
I know you could have
if you only wanted to."
she kissed Me last night.
Long, soft and empty.
At least it seemed on her end.
Empty, hungry, wanting. Sad.
I could fill her up with promise,
If she only wanted Me to.

This Much I Do Know

I love you.
I long for you,
weeping constantly
as a widow mourns
the loss of her husband.
I have no appetite for food;
sweet sleep eludes Me.
Every breath aches with sobbing.
My eyes are blind,
burned by their own ceaseless tears.
My future is uncertain,
but one thing I am sure of;
I love you.

To Catch a Butterfly

There is something about a butterfly
that makes you stop
what you are doing,
stand soldier still,
with stifled breath
until it feels safe enough
to alight on something nearby.
What about such a delicate, peaceful creature
makes us silently pray,
" Please land on me."
To catch a butterfly,
you must be steadfast as a tree,
flexible as a reed,
gentle as a rose petal,
and as nourishing as rain.
Only then will it trust you enough
to rest on your arm.

There is something about you
that makes Me want to drop everything,
stand soldier still
with captured breath,
until you believe that I love you.
Something in you,
beautiful, incredible woman,
makes Me pray,
" Please trust in Me."

To win your heart,
I will be steadfast as a tree,
flexible as a reed,
gentle as a rose petal,
and as nourishing as rain.
Perhaps then you will trust Me enough
to rest in My arms.

Tunnel Vision

In the Cosmic blackness
teeming with fireflies,
I gaze through this concept man calls Time,
into your effervescent eyes.
My soul sees through you,
My heart laid bare;
asking of you nothing more
than the return of My stare.
Out here no sound would dare corrupt
the crispness of your laughter,
but the silence of promise
of Love ever after.
But bereft of your presence,
denied of your light;
what good are the stars
in the blackness of night?

Upon My Pedestal

From way up here on My pedestal,
where she put Me,
I can see the whole world.
Over the mountains I can see the ocean.
Through the clouds I can see the sun shining.
And it shines brightest way up here
on My pedestal.
From way up here I can hear the stars whisper.
No one else can do that.
From way up here,
where she holds Me prisoner,
I can hear the grass grow.
I can hear the birds sing,
and they sing loudest
way up here on My pedestal.
I am up here because she saw fit that I should be.
she put Me up here like a hero.
But I am not a hero.
Heroes never get scared.
So, here I am; a scared hero.
Way up here, higher than the stars,
higher than the sun and the moon,
higher than God.
Afraid that I might fall,
but even more scared that one day
she might take Me down from way up here
On My pedestal.

View of the Sky from the Garden

I lie solitary in the garden at night.
My loneliness
is a deep indigo blue,
vast and eternal.
you are a single pin-point star,
a trillion light years away from Me.
I see you,
I believe in your existence,
but I fear that in My short lifetime,
I will never be able to reach you.
You are so bright,
so amazing,
so incredible.
It is no wonder, then,
that I am not worthy of touching you.

Wasted

When you come to Me so softly,
gliding across the floor,
weightless,
My heart explodes
with the fullness of Love
I hold for you.
My throat tightens
as I hold back
the tears that come
from My fear of one day
waking up without you.
My hand reaches for you,
pulling you close,
faster, so you get here sooner.
I can't let one
second go by,
wasted,
because I didn't touch you.

What Magic?

To have My mind's eye
forever seeing only you;
to hold My heart so,
as though a chain were run clean through;
to capture My soul
and hold it furious and fast;
I must entreat you,
"What manner of spell have you cast??

Can lightening compare
to the power in your kiss?
Do shooting stars dare
disturb the moment of our bliss?
When the moon is full,
lighting all the skies above,
I gaze at your face and ask,
" What magic has this love?"

Will We?

When we are old
will you help Me pick berries?
Will we teach our grandkids
to believe in good Faeries?

When I am gray
will you play with My hair;
touch My smile-wrinkled cheek;
blow a kiss in the air?

When you are frail,
may I help you be strong?
Will you let Me be with you
your whole lifetime long?

And when we are free
of this Earth-body tether,
may I hold your soul with Me
forever and ever?

My insides flutter with desire.
I am trembling.
Basking in your Love,
I become
the butterflies.

What is desire
but the mind afire,
and Love a vast forest
willingly burning?

She enchants my spirit,
willing it to laugh.
I am unveiled before her,
my soul bare.

Moon and Stars

I had just a hint
of the sweetness
that could come my way
if I play
My cards right.

I saw just a glimpse
of the magic,
that was held in your kiss;
the delicious bliss
as we said goodnight.

I wished on a star;
danced on the moon
that shone in your eyes
and lit up the skies.
That made everything right.

Absolute Jewel

As close as skin allows
for face to be next to heart,
you lay your head down and hear me
breathing with your sighs

About the Author

From early in her childhood, Karen Godson has had a strong will to be right, and to be in charge. She admits that she loves to be noticed, and still fondly remembers winning a place in the Peel Region School Board's Poetry Anthology at the age of eight, with her poem called "The Runaway".

Karen now works as a "pen for hire", while continuing to write poetry and other short stories, both kinky and "Vanilla". She chooses to write under her real name, declaring, "If I'm not proud enough to stand behind my work, then maybe it isn't worth publishing."

www.ingramcontent.com/pod-product-compliance
Lightning Source LLC
Chambersburg PA
CBHW081022040426

42444CB00014B/3321